June 16, 1993

I will always "Love" you.

HAPPY ANNIVERSARY

A How To Book for Husbands and Wives

Written By:
Herbert Kavet

Illustrated By:
Martin Riskin

Manufactured in the United States of America

30 29 28 27 26 25 24 23 22 21 20 19 18 17 16 15 14 13 12 11 10 9 8 7 6 5 4 3 2

Ivory Tower Publishing Co., Inc.
125 Walnut St., Watertown, MA 02172
Telephone #: (617) 923-1111 Fax #: (617) 923-8839

ACKNOWLEDGMENT

This book was conceived while sailing in the Greek Islands with two other couples and my wife. After a week, the husbands discovered that all their wives need lots of improvement. Simultaneously, the wives discovered the same thing (about their husbands -- not themselves). Dave Barry correctly described the problem, "Marriages generally involve males and females, who are not called opposite sexes for nothing."

Thanks to Kelly, Chiara, Karen, Ronnie, and Nico for the ideas, and I hope you all can improve before the next trip.

A Russian friend of mine told about a division of responsibility that he had with his wife. She took care of all the little decisions: where to live, what car to buy, when to vacation, what to eat, how the children should be educated, etc. He took care of all the big decisions: should Russia and the U.S. sign a disarmament treaty, who should be present at a Mideast peace conference, should the industrialized countries aid starving Africans, and who should control the ozone layer and the Rain Forests.

It worked beautifully.

WHAT WIVES WANT OUT OF MARRIAGE

There is always room to improve a husband. Don't believe that stuff about women being made from Adam's rib. More likely little girls <u>are</u> made from sugar and spice and everything nice and boys from puppy dog tails.

Wives want:

1. Romance
2. Love and Respect
3. A Bloomingdale's Charge Card

"YOO HOO, CLIFFORD."

Men want:

1. To be left alone when watching football games
2. A partner who doesn't notice the beer belly or protruding nose hair
3. To be allowed to go right to sleep after sex

Are you tired of a husband who is too short or who sucks raspberry seeds from his teeth after dinner? How about a husband who stinks up the bathroom on a daily basis and has even more disgusting personal habits that you've never even mentioned in public? Does your husband's mind lie in the gutter and that's a step up from his TV tastes, and is his body starting to be shaped like a beer bottle?

Why bother with disruptive trade-ins. This book will give you solid tips for improving the model you're already stuck with.

"MY HUSBAND ADDED SOME MAGIC TO OUR MARRIAGE— HE DISAPPEARED."

Are you trying to get your wife to exercise a bit to melt off some cellulite? How about those futile efforts to develop her interests in healthy, exciting activities like football, fishing, or racing cars? Are you anxious to get her mind off hair spray and soap operas and into a Chinese cooking or massage class?

Don't risk potentially expensive alterations to your marital status. This book will teach you all you need to remold the one you already have.

There is probably practically no truth to the theory that women's brains are fried due to their excessive use of hair dryers. Why, even some men use hair dryers, but, of course, not nearly as frequently as women.

Most male doctors think women's brains shrink from washing their hair ten times a week.

JAQUELINE IS ALMOST POSITIVE THAT HOROSCOPES ARE TOTAL BUNK.

Your husband's brain is inversely proportional to the amount of time he spends thinking about his sex organs. If he thinks about his penis all day long, he's going to have a very stunted brain indeed. Many husbands think it is worth it.

To improve your husband's brain, you have to think of some way to get his mind off sex -- Good luck!

Almost all women think their breasts are too small. Feed her the old baloney about anything more than a handful is wasted. She won't believe you, but the thought will make her happier.

WIVES KNOW THAT ANYTHING MORE THAN A HANDFUL IS WASTED.

A happy husband is a husband who thinks he has the longest, thickest penis in the whole world. Tell him so, often. Few grown men go around measuring other guys' penises in locker rooms. They really have no idea what's big or small so he'll believe whatever you say and be happy and will come home every night to hear about it again.

ENCOURAGING YOUR HUSBAND TO GET IN TOUCH WITH HIS EMOTIONS

1. Teach him that it is permissible for men to cry.
2. Explain that caring and sensitivity and affection are much more important than sex.
3. This will make almost any man cry.

"OF COURSE I'LL RESPECT YOU IN THE MORNING."

1. Patiently explain that she feels this way each month.
2. Let her cry all she wants.
3. Tell her she still looks slim.
4. Let her eat all the chocolate and salt she wants.
5. Try to be out of town.

1. Spend ridiculous amounts of time on foreplay.
2. Keep repeating how much you love her.
3. Try to hold back till she's had a turn.
4. Rub her back afterwards rather than immediately going to sleep.
5. Talk about love for a long, long time.

"YOU KNOW EXACTLY WHAT I MEANT BY A 'MENAGE A TROIS'!"

1. Go ahead and dress up in one of those ridiculous outfits.
2. Pretend to climax with him.
3. Bounce around a lot near the end.
4. Agree to "do it" if you can gargle afterwards.
5. Tell him it was the best ever.

"WE'VE BEEN THINKING ABOUT GROUP SEX."

IMPROVING YOUR HUSBAND'S BATHROOM HABITS

Bathrooms are the world's leading cause of divorce. It's just hard to keep loving someone after seeing parts of their bodies on various porcelain surfaces.

These five hints may take the edge off some of your husband's more annoying traits:

1. Insist he pick his hair off the soap.
2. Explain what the stick with the brush that's next to the toilet is for.
3. Drill him on lowering the toilet seat.
4. Have him rinse away the little shaving hairs.
5. Make him clean his comb and brush once a year.

1. Convince her to put the kitty litter in the back hallway.
2. Consolidate the Midol, Advil, and Pamprin into one large cabinet.
3. Explain how the cap is screwed onto the top of the toothpaste.
4. Limit the shampoo bottles, including conditioners, to 4 shelves.
5. Set up a reservation system so you can get some mirror time in the mornings.

IMPROVING YOUR WIFE'S BATHROOM HABITS

There are only four places to hide vegetables that you don't like:

1. Slip them onto a cooperating husband's or wife's plate.
2. Bury them in the mashed potatoes.
3. Wrap them in a napkin and leave it by someone else's chair.
4. Instigate a food fight and use them as ammunition.

My wife plays with her food. She has always played with her food. I know because I asked her mother. It's not so much of a problem at home but it's hell in a restaurant. You can never get a waiter to bring the next course and when the meal is over, you can't get a check. Your ass is numb, your feet have fallen asleep, and everyone is anxious to go to bed, but every time the waiter looks over, my wife is moving a string bean or diddling a microscopic piece of fish with her fork.

Write if you have any suggestions.

"MADAME, YOU HAVE SMALL CHILDREN AT HOME, N'EST PA?"

HOW TO KEEP YOUR WIFE FROM LOSING YOUR SOCKS

There is no way to keep a wife from losing socks in the laundry. I try to buy only one or two colors of the same socks, and this cuts my losses since I can occasionally get a match.

I'm convinced that no woman can get into heaven until she has accounted for every lost sock.

Husbands never understand why you can't mix white and colored laundry. There is some sort of genetic brain block that prevents husbands from learning this.

If you yell at your husband about the pinkish tinge in all your white things, he will only get angry, deny it, and never use the washing machine again.

HOW TO IMPROVE YOUR WIFE'S GOLF GAME

1. Offer to carry your own bag.
2. Don't be stingy with lessons if the pro is young and cute.
3. Agree to play without keeping score.
4. Allow her two Mulligans per hole.
5. Take up tennis.

1. Bend over when his opponent is about to putt.
2. Let him add up all the scores.
3. Encourage him to play with older women.
4. Look away when he moves his ball to a better lie.
5. Take up modern dance.

"IRMA IS WORKING THE DISTRACTION GAME FOR ALL IT'S WORTH TODAY."

17

1. When you come home from work, bring a feather. Undress your wife and slowly rub the feather all over her body, tickling and teasing her. It will drive her crazy.
2. When you come back from shopping, bring some whipped cream and strawberries. Undress your wife and spread the whipped cream all over her body, using a strawberry as a special garnish. Lick it all off. It will drive her crazy.
3. When you come home all greasy and dirty from working on your car or in the yard, undress your wife and make love to her in whatever room you find her. Wipe your hands on the curtains. It will drive her crazy.

TESTING YOUR WIFE
HUSBAND - "Darling, if I passed away, would you remarry?"
WIFE - "Well, I guess so."
HUSBAND - "Would the two of you sleep in our bed?"
WIFE - "I suppose we would if we lived here."
HUSBAND - "Would you have sex with him?"
WIFE - "Sweety, he would be my husband."
HUSBAND - "Would you give him my new golf club?"
WIFE - "No. He's left-handed."
"A MARRIAGE WILL ONLY WORK WHEN BOTH PARTIES ARE TOTALLY HONEST WITH EACH OTHER."

GETTING YOUR WIFE TO DIET

Never start by telling her she's jiggling when she brushes her teeth or that her behind oozes through the straps when she sits in a lawn chair.

It's better to say:

1. No. No. I don't think you're gaining weight. Those toilet seats break all the time. They're made of cheap plastic these days.
2. Nellie Sneider was on the Stairmaster with this lycra outfit. All the guys thought she was a teenager.
3. Myrna lost 22 lbs. in one week with the new fig diet.

GETTING YOUR HUSBAND TO DIET

Calling your husband lard belly and trying to substitute celery for potato chips is only going to harden his resistance.

Better you should say:

1. Harry Garfinkle bought a new bike and he's training to ride across France this summer.
2. Smitty runs all the way to work when the weather is good. Yep, 63 miles each way. Can eat anything he likes.
3. Muffy showed me this article about thin men having a higher testosterone level.

Need a few simple gimmicks for getting your husband to a culturally enriching film?

1. Tell him it's R rated and has steamy sex.
2. Tell him there's a nude scene with a body he won't believe.
3. Tell him it's so scary that you need someone brave to sit next to.

Do you need a simple rule to get your wife to a film that doesn't put you to sleep in the first 15 minutes?

1. Tell her you heard it shows the most meaningful, sensitive, romantic scenes.
2. Tell her your partner's wife cried through the whole movie.
3. Tell her her mother made you promise not to take her.

There are three kinds of poor drivers:

1. Too fast drivers
2. Too slow drivers
3. Drivers who look at you when they talk to you even if you're sitting in the back seat

Handling Fast Drivers - You scream at them, "Sidney, you're doing 95!"

Handling Slow Drivers - Say in your most exasperated form: "The speed limit is 35."

You haven't known true terror until you get a really polite or somewhat insecure driver who feels he or she has to look at you while they're talking. You know the kind. They want to be sure you're listening or agreeing to whatever they're saying. This becomes nightmare type fear when they are the ones supposed to be driving. About the only thing you can do is pretend to fall asleep so they will stop talking to you.

HOW TO GET YOUR HUSBAND TO ASK FOR DIRECTIONS

There is this lodge or fraternity, if you will, that all men belong to. One of its main rules is that real men never ever ask for directions. That's why, even if your husband is hopelessly lost in a terrible neighborhood or without a map, he insists on bumbling around rather than seeking help. Should he stop at a gas station for directions, he will be instantly reported to the club headquarters (somewhere in Kansas) and be immediately excommunicated.

The only way to get your husband to ask for directions is to get special dispensation, before a trip, from the Grand Lodge Master by swearing your man is hopelessly dyslexic.

You can also yell "help" when you pass a policeman.

Wives will always ask for directions even when they're not lost. Some wives ask so many directions that they never really get anyplace.

FIVE WAYS TO HELP YOUR HUSBAND BUY A CAR

ALL NEW
SPITZ 5000

1. Never let him go to the showroom alone.
2. Never let him deal with a saleswoman with bigger boobs than yours.
3. Never let him deal with a saleswoman.
4. Constantly remind him that the car has to also hold three kids and a dog.
5. Remember that all men played with toy trucks and racing cars as children and have never outgrown it.

Wives don't have disgusting habits. They have annoying ones.

1. Reading newspaper articles to you at breakfast
2. Humming or laughing as they read in bed
3. "Oh my"ing when watching TV
4. Keeping a foot on the brake when they drive
5. Nibbling the edges of cake just to even them out

While you can't really eliminate these annoying habits, you can control them by distracting her with one of your disgusting habits.

HANDLING YOUR WIFE'S ANNOYING HABITS

HANDLING YOUR HUSBAND'S DISGUSTING HABITS

Husbands often exhibit some or all of the following disgusting personal habits:

1. Farting
2. Nose picking
3. Cleaning ears
4. Scratching you-know-where
5. Burping

It is common knowledge that women never commit these loathsome traits even after eating Mexican food or drinking beer. No woman, to the best of my knowledge, has ever farted.

It's a wife's job to say, "Oooh that's disgusting" whenever her husband does them.

"LIONEL DOESN'T CONSIDER FARTING RUDE SINCE HIS DOCTOR RECOMMENDED THE BROCCOLI."

GETTING YOUR HUSBAND TO SHAVE BEFORE SEX

1. Show the whisker burns to your mother.
2. Stop shaving your own mustache.
3. Soften his chin with dabs of Vaseline until he gets the hint.

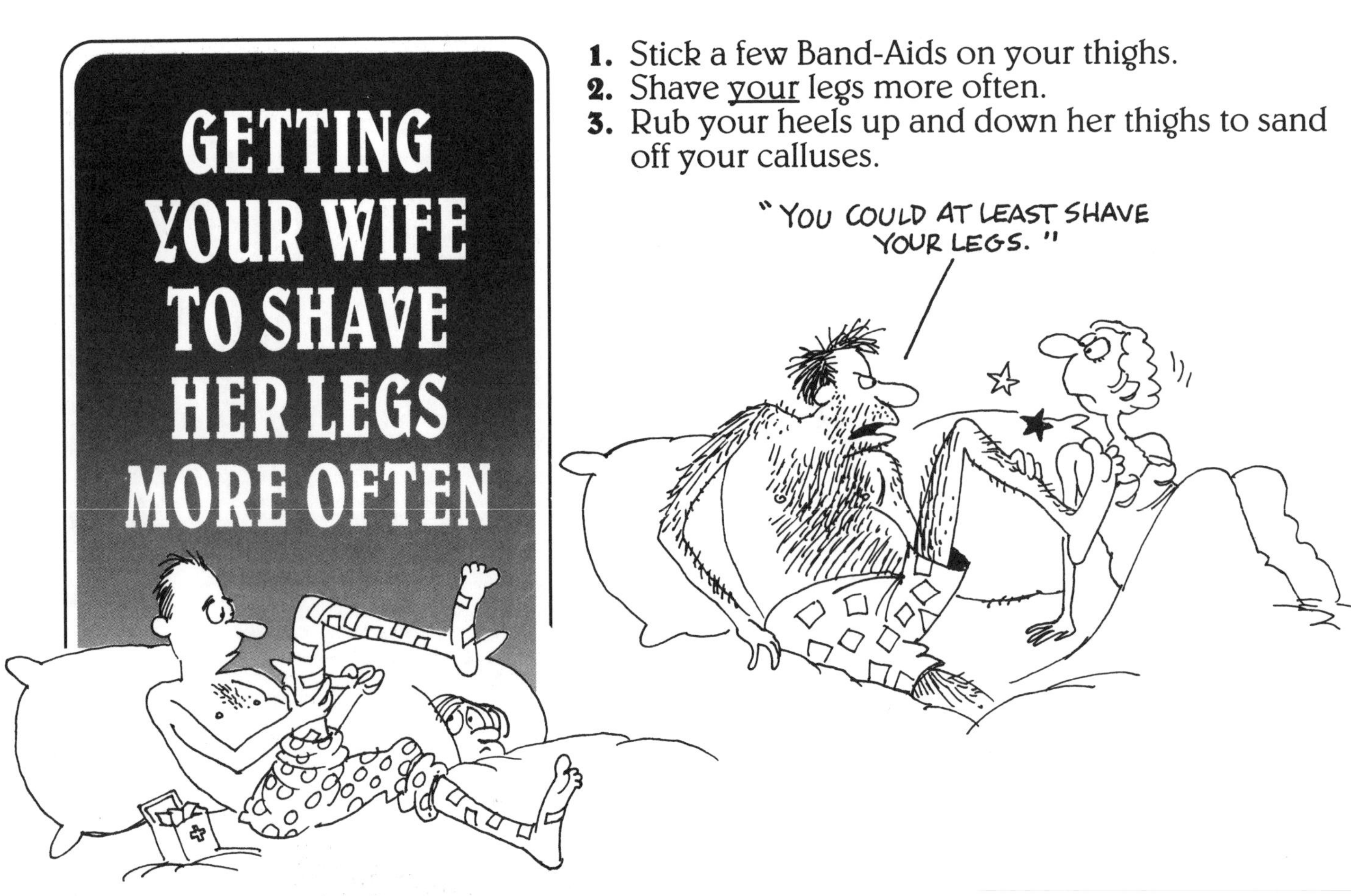

1. Stick a few Band-Aids on your thighs.
2. Shave your legs more often.
3. Rub your heels up and down her thighs to sand off your calluses.

FIVE WAYS TO HELP YOUR WIFE BUY A CAR

1. Never let her go to a showroom alone.
2. Be suspicious of any salesman who treats her as an equal.
3. Don't explain about valves and camshafts and suspensions because then she'll realize you don't know what they are, either.
4. Insist that "cute" is never a good reason to buy a car.
5. Always let her choose the color.

The best way to get your wife to do this erotic and sensual treat is to reward her. Reward her in cash as they do in Middle Eastern Restaurants around the world.

Stuff dollar bills down her bra and pants.

With proper instruction, even the most bumbling husband can be taught to clean a toilet. It's only a matter of the proper motivation. Husbands plead ignorance over this simple task to avoid an unpleasant job. Some wives try to outwait their husbands and just let the bathroom get gross. This doesn't work, since men can simply tolerate more filth.

You teach husbands to clean a toilet by letting the toilet paper run out, and only bringing them a roll if they promise to clean up.

HOW TO IMPROVE YOUR HUSBAND IN THE MORNING

Morning problems can be divided into two categories:

1. Breath
2. Disposition

There is no way to improve either.

YOU FEEL LIKE THE MORNING AFTER AND YOU CAN SWEAR YOU HAVEN'T BEEN ANYWHERE.

1. Get him to wear a more flattering shade of lipstick.
2. Encourage a bushy beard that covers the offending parts.
3. Clip all protruding nose hairs.
4. Suggest a liposuction procedure for his nose.

1. Teach her to use a straight edge razor so she can get a real close shave.
2. Take a paper bag and cut out holes for the eyes, nose and mouth.
3. Bring home a giant tube of Clearasil.
4. Get her to breathe through her nose so her teeth won't show.

Just kidding, ladies.

HOW TO STOP YOUR WIFE FROM BEING A CHEAPSKATE

Most wives are not cheapskates. Au contraire, they spend a vastly disproportionate percentage of the family income and that mostly on two commodities: shampoo and conditioner. It's a fact that over 58% of the average household budget goes for a bewildering (to any male) array of the most imaginatively packaged soap you have ever seen. The number of colorful and cleverly shaped plastic bottles that a wife acquires is limited only by the load-bearing capacity of the bathroom walls. God knows the stuff works. Women seldom go bald.

There was this husband who was so cheap that he had his vasectomy done at Sears. Every time he got an erection, the garage door went up.

You explain to a cheapskate husband that you only go around once in this life and if he doesn't spend it, you'll only be using it to party with your next husband.

Since there is no way to improve your mate's breath or disposition, it's best to just stay away from each other until you've brushed your teeth and had your coffee.

MAKE YOUR WIFE SEEM MORE INTERESTING AT A PARTY

1. Allude to her quest to regain her virginity.
2. Refuse to tell what she really did at Woodstock.
3. Infer that she worked as a sex slave in the Catskills before you were married.
4. Hint about her insatiable curiosity concerning kinky sex.
5. Hint about her insatiable desires for coffee heathbar crunch ice cream.

1. Drop an innuendo about his Mob connections.
2. Suggest that his business trips involve the CIA.
3. Confide to one friend that he lived with a homosexual in college.
4. Imply that he keeps a mistress.
5. Be very knowledgeable about impotence.

MAKE YOUR HUSBAND SEEM MORE INTERESTING AT A PARTY

SPENDING QUALITY TIME WITH YOUR WIFE'S FAMILY

1. Move far away.
2. Have two stiff drinks before they arrive.
3. Identify the family fool or blacksheep (never a difficult task) and befriend this person.

Husbands come up with the most ridiculous projects and ideas. Since most never get beyond the talking stage, it's really silly to get all worked up over each one. Better save your time and just ignore them.

The following expressions make it easy:

1. Uh huh.
2. That's a wonderful idea.
3. Of course I'm listening.

HOW TO IGNORE YOUR WIFE

Sometimes you simply can't improve your wife. When this happens, many men choose to ignore their wife, instead. Some husbands have developed this to such a high level that they don't even realize that they still have wives.

To learn this skill, practice with the following expressions:

1. Uh Huh.
2. Yes, dear.
3. Of course I heard what you said.

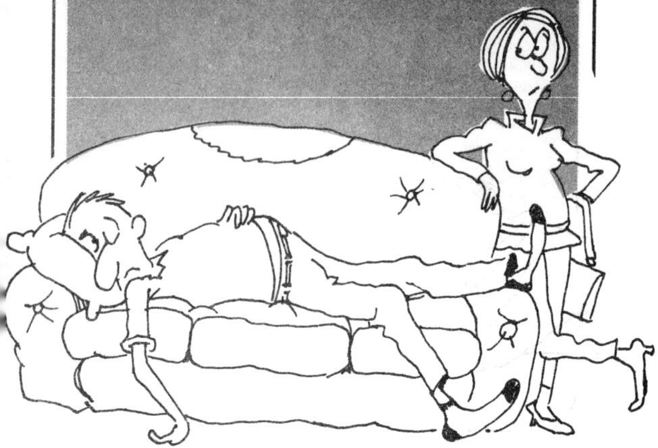

All wives diet and this often leads to a caloric deficiency that makes them irritable and hard to live with. Increase her happiness with the following caloric guidelines.

Calories don't count if:

1. You add beansprouts.
2. You're only evening out the edges of a cake.
3. You're just tasting.
4. Oat bran is one of the ingredients.
5. Someone's mother baked it.

A happy wife is a good wife, and you can increase your wife's happiness by making her diets more fun. Forget that stuff about leafy vegetables, skim milk and lima beans. Food theories change every few years anyway. Simply make sure she covers the basics with the following food groups:

Eat at least three portions each day from the five main dessert groups:

1. New York Cheesecake
2. Coffee Heath Bar Crunch Ice Cream
3. Lemon Iced Carrot Cake
   (can also count as a vegetable)
4. Chocolate Mousse and Whipped Cream
5. Homemade Chocolate Chip Peanut Butter Cookies

It is permissible to add hot fudge to any of the above if she is suffering from a PMS chocolate craving.

See if the time spent qualifies for college credits in an anthropology or sociology course. Husbands' families are often great thesis material. If this is not practical, feign an allergic reaction to an animal, plant or rug at their house.

IMPROVING YOUR HUSBAND'S DIET

The latest studies show that dangers from heart attacks, cancer, and everything can be reduced by drinking. Be sure your husband takes two belts from the following group each day:

1. Sam Adams, Budweiser, or Heineken beer
2. California Chardonnay
3. A Scotch whiskey claiming to be older than your children
4. Any vodka with a Russian sounding name you can't pronounce
5. Thick Italian liquors that are mixed with soda

Note -- any alcohol consumed during a cocktail hour does not count if your husband had a stressful day.

Snacks are important for between meal energy. Every husband who watches TV for more than three hours a day should be offered two meals from this food group:

1. Kettle cooked potato chips
2. Microwave popcorn
3. Salted nuts
4. Pretzels (must be combined with a beer to qualify)
5. Barbecue flavored corn chips

When we go out, my wife warns me about the politics and causes of the people we will be with and admonishes me not to talk about those things or sex or bodily functions or any of the good information she has on who has been arrested, is having an affair, or is about to divorce.

Then she wonders why I sit alone all evening and have a lousy time.

Any man married more than three years knows weekends are best for sex. Weeknights should be reserved for resting up for tomorrow. If your wife becomes romantic during the week, one of the following remarks will probably change her mind:

1. Of course I love you, I'm your husband, that's my job.
2. I think the kids are listening.
3. Great idea. Get your leather stockings and I'll oil up the gorilla suit.
4. Sure honey, the doctor said the bladder infection probably isn't contagious.
5. What did you say your name is?

1. Wearing hair curlers to bed
2. Always using flannel nighties
3. Headaches
4. That time of the month
5. Asking - "Is it in yet?"

1. Insist he look both ways before running a red light.
2. Close your eyes when he makes a U-turn on a crowded street so your screaming won't distract him.
3. Look nonchalant when he gives the finger to other drivers but nevertheless, roll up the window.

Teach her the following:

1. To use the horn aggressively. This produces less wear and tear on your car as well as being a more efficient way to move your auto.
2. To never signal when making a left-hand turn from the right-hand lane. It warns the other drivers and gives them a chance to honk their horn at her.
3. To zip through corner gas stations to avoid the traffic stopped by a red light.

Never, never talk about:

1. The number of times he gets up to pee each night.
2. The fact it takes him all night to do what he used to do all night.
3. The way he massages his balding spot for ten minutes each morning.
4. How he still sleeps with his teddy bear.

A wife is surprised by her husband's early return. Thinking quickly, she shoves his best friend into the closet and lies moaning on the bed as her husband comes in. "Oooh - I think I'm having a heart attack." The husband runs frantically for a phone and bumps into his four-year-old who is crying, "There's a man in Mommy's closet." The husband tears open the closet and sees his naked friend. "For Pete's sake, Sam. Marsha is having a heart attack and all you can do is scare the kids."

This is not easy. Wives read all those women's magazines which give figures on infidelity. What's happening is that 90% of all men are giving us other 10% a bad name.

The actual making of coffee is not what proves difficult to most husbands. It's finding the little paper filters that screws them up. Leave the filters out on the counter, and while the result may be strong enough to float a spoon or so weak as to resemble apple juice, at least you won't be bothered.

Here's how women use a thermostat. Say it's set at 70 degrees and they're cold so they put it up to maybe 90 degrees so it will get warm fast. Then when they find they're too hot, they put it down to 55 degrees so it will get colder fast.

Their logic is intuitively obvious and women as an intuitive sex cannot be taught any other method of using a thermostat.

Every night before making love say:

1. "I love you. I love you. I love you."
2. "Oooh. It's so tight."
3. "I could keep this up forever."
4. "I promise to sleep on the wet spot."

1. "Are you done yet?"
2. "Everyone else does it."
3. "What's that smell?"
4. "You're doing it wrong."

WHAT TO SAY TO MAKE YOUR WIFE MORE INSECURE

WHAT TO SAY TO MAKE YOUR HUSBAND MORE SECURE

1. "You're hurting me. Ohmygod, don't stop don't stop."
2. "Yes, yes, six times."
3. "I've never seen anything so enormous."

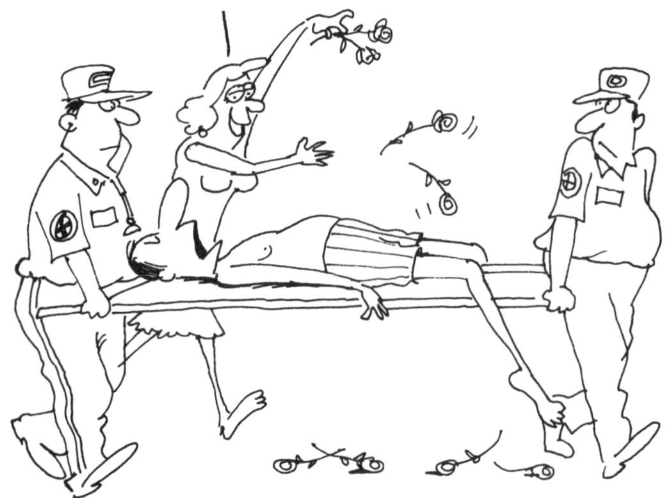

You can make any husband insecure by saying:

1. "Isn't that cute."
2. "Don't think you can just go to sleep now."
3. "I didn't think men got cellulite."
4. "Just leave it on the dresser."

1. Trade him for someone else's husband.
2. Turn off the lights and as soon as he falls asleep, (usually no long wait) sneak out to the local hangout.
3. Agree to do the crisco and rubber sheet bit if he cleans up afterwards.

Do you know what it means to come home to a husband who gives you a little love, a little consideration, a little tenderness? It means you're in the wrong house.

1. Bring home some ridiculous (at her present body weight) sexy lingerie.
2. Convince her your kinky fantasies are really innocent idiosyncrasies.
3. Pretend to believe her when she fakes an orgasm.

Before you can do this you have to explain how a car works. Here's how. A car is made up of thousands (some say millions) of funny little parts all jumbled and greasy inside. When you pour gasoline in one end and light a spark, some of the parts catch fire and jiggle around and make the car move.

These parts jiggling is all well and good but sometimes one of the billions (maybe there are billions of them) of the little parts break. The car tells you something is wrong by making a funny noise. It will usually make this noise only when you are driving alone and never ever when you take it to a real mechanic. The trick to fixing cars is to get the car to make the noise at a service station.

Good luck. I usually just sell my car when these noises start.

MAKING YOUR HUSBAND OR WIFE A BETTER MECHANIC

Husbands are very good for fixing flat tires, washing and waxing cars and retrieving lipsticks that roll under the seats.

Asking your husband to do anything else to your car will only void the warranty.

DOUGLAS FINALLY OWNS A CAR THAT IS TOTALLY PAID FOR.

Three friends are drinking at their favorite bar when one confesses he's always really been a woman trapped in a man's body and tomorrow he's going for a sex change operation. A month later the new woman is recovered and is recounting the experience. Her friends ask "about the operation."

"Was the worst part the part when they cut off your balls and penis?" "No, that wasn't too bad," she answered. "I'll bet it was when they made the artificial vagina," said the other. "Naw, that was o.k." "How about the breast implanting?" "No," she said, "The only bad part was when they cut my salary in half."

"THAT EXPLAINS THE DIFFERENCE IN OUR SALARIES."

It's easy. You can even control the cost of keeping her well dressed. Just use one of the following comments to discourage an outfit that is expensive or inappropriate.

1. It makes you look, well, mature.
2. Your figure seems fuller in it.
3. You'll never have to worry about being carded.
4. The draping calls attention to your hips.
5. The color gives your skin a swarthy texture.

Men's clothes can be divided into upper and lower body garments.

To dispose of ugly trousers, simply say, "It looks baggy in the crotch." No husband wants to walk around with a baggy crotch and since he can't really see the crotch himself, he will believe you and never wear the pants again.

For upper body stuff you'd prefer he dispose of, just say, "It makes you look a little heavy," and be ready to take it to the Salvation Army collection point on Monday morning.

TEACHING YOUR WIFE ABOUT PLUMBING

All wives have a natural proclivity for white porcelain surfaces and any plumbing operation involving sinks, toilets and washing machines should be left to them. If you'd rather not mess with these things, flushing a few diapers down the toilet with a shrug and "I didn't know you were supposed to hold on to it with your HAND" will convince them. You can also put a little extra detergent in the washing machine and the resulting foam will probably cause her to ban you from the laundry room.

Stuffed up toilets and overflowing septic systems are definitely men's jobs. Establish this early in your marriage by using your husband's #2 wood, or a fishing rod to unstuff a toilet. He will insist on doing the job himself after that.

Any job that involves disconnecting pipes is best left to a real plumber if you value your marriage.

All parents want their children to marry someone of the same religion. They also prefer marriages to someone of exactly the same ethnic, class and social background, though being lots richer is o.k. If your husband is of a different religion, your parents will always bug you to get him to convert. His parents likewise are probably bugging him to get you to convert. The solution is simple. You convert to his religion and he converts to your religion and then both sets of in-laws should be satisfied.

Getting people to change their religion is always tough and what you probably need is a miracle. Miracles are always good for opening people's minds on religion. One excellent miracle is a simultaneous orgasm.

GET YOUR HUSBAND TO BRING HIS OWN SHIRTS TO THE LAUNDRY

WONG's WASH 'n WAIT

"Honey," he cried. "This shirt collar is too tight. I can hardly breathe. This can't be my shirt. The laundry must have mixed them up."

"No, that's your shirt alright," said his wife. "You just have your head through the button hole."

GET YOUR WIFE TO CHECK THE OIL IN HER CAR

I went through three engines on one station wagon and still couldn't get my kids to check the oil. I'm not the person to teach you how to get your wife to do this simple job.

A husband should have a complete physical every year. One fellow came back from his examination and told his wife that the doctor wanted him to return with a urine specimen, a stool smear, and a semen sample. His wife said, "That's easy. Just bring him a pair of your underpants."

Your husband is too fat when:

1. He starts leaving footprints in the hardwood floors.
2. He turns off the lights before undressing.
3. He yells at you for shrinking his jeans.

1. Set the mood early with refined acts of kindness as soon as you come home.
2. Discuss meaningful ways in which you relate to each other.
3. Talk endlessly about love.
4. Engage in lengthy but sensitive foreplay.
5. Never ever rate the performance on a scale of 1 - 10.

Touching, kissing, communicating, rubbing, caressing, undressing, sighing, squeezing, and fondling are all important preludes to lovemaking. Train your husband to spend time on them by insisting he keep his shorts on for 15 minutes from the time he first bounces up and down on the bed.

Explain that staring at your breasts, parading nude in front of the mirror while holding his stomach in and unzipping his fly while talking about how big it is does not constitute adequate foreplay.

Year 1	For the first year of marriage you ignore him.
Year 2-5	You scream, "Aarrgh - that's disgusting."
After Year 5	You blow him out of the bed with your own farts.

Year 1	During the first year of marriage, you don't notice. You think it's your powerful lovemaking.
Year 2-5	You can't believe a woman could do such a thing. You assume the kids are making some sort of noise.
After Year 5	You are already asleep.

A HOBBY FOR YOUR HUSBAND OR WIFE

There is probably too much leisure time in our world. I mean look at some of the stupid things people get involved in. What sane person collects old hub caps, watches birds or sews a quilt to cover the barn?

All hobbies can be divided into three groups:

1. Weird hobbies
2. Dumb hobbies
3. Your hobbies

A person's own hobby can be further divided:

1. People less fanatical than you - turkeys
2. People more fanatical than you - assholes

For true marital happiness it's good to encourage a spouse to get involved in a practical hobby. A wife who learns to brew beer is always appreciated, as is a skilled handyman husband who can build shelves (to hold more shampoo).

1. Take long walks together.
2. Talk of romance every night at dinner.
3. Watch sensitive movies and TV.
4. Find activities you can share like gardening and photography.
5. Cut off the sex until he gives you long back rubs in the morning.

1. Explain why you have to punt on the 4th down.
2. Teach her to ski and play baseball.
3. Help develop her taste for guzzling beer.
4. Illustrate the practical advantages of owning a Porche 911.
5. Always hold the door open when she takes out the garbage.